North American
F-108 Rapier

Hugh Harkins

North American
F-108 Rapier

© Hugh Harkins 2014

Createspace Independent Publishing Platform

ISBN 10: 1497577926
ISBN 13: 978-1497577923

This volume first published 2014

The Publishers and Author would like to thank all organisations and services for their assistance and contributions in the preparation of this volume

CONTENTS

INTRODUCTION

Designed as a Mach 3 high altitude interceptor during the late 1950's, the North American F-108 was at the pinnacle of aircraft design during the period. The aircraft, like its larger stable mate, the North American XB-70 strategic bomber, was, however, ultimately doomed due to high costs and a looming redundancy due to a shifting strategic threat in the shape of Inter-Continental Ballistic Missiles, which were then on the cusp of taking over the mantle of strategic nuclear strike from manned bombers.

This volume looks at the genesis and development of the various iterations of the F-108A from the program inception to beyond its cancellation in 1959. The volume is supported by a number of photographs, technical drawings and planned performance charts.

1

TOWARDS A MACH 3 INTERCEPTOR

The North American F-108 Rapier was designed as a Mach 3 high altitude interceptor capable of intercepting projected 1960's advanced Soviet bombers that could be expected to attack North America in the event that the Cold War turned hot. It is often claimed that the aircraft was also to be capable of escorting the North American B-70 Valkyrie Mach 3 strategic bomber then under development for the USAF (United States Air Force) SAC (Strategic Air Command), however, this latter role is not supported by available documents.

The fear of nuclear attack against the United States by Soviet bomber aircraft led to interceptors assuming a prominent role in continental air defense as the world moved into the era of superpower stand-off and arms race which commenced in the years immediately following the end of World War II. From the late 1940's, the air defense of North America had assumed an urgent priority and by the early 1950's several subsonic interceptor types, such as the Northrop F-98 Scorpion, Lockheed F-94 Starfire and North American F-86D, were in service, and the development of supersonic interceptors was being urgently pressed on with, in particular the MX-1554 so called 'Ultimate Interceptor', or the '1954 Interceptor' (denoting the planned in service year) that would lead to the Convair F-102 Delta Dagger, which suffered a myriad of development problems. These problems ultimately delayed service entry until 1956; the build-up of operational F-102 squadrons being swift, with some 25 ADC (Air Defense Command) squadrons equipped with the type at the peak of service in the late 1950's.

Even as this generation of interceptors was being developed attention was turning to the projected post 1960 threat that was expected to be faced from advanced Soviet bomber aircraft. These projected threats led to the LRI-X (Long Range-Interceptor Experimental) program that would eventually lead to the F-108 program.

Conceived in the climate of fear that was the Cold War in the 1950's, the F-108 was developed at a time when the threat it was designed to counter was actually receding in magnitude in comparison to the new threat of ICBM (Inter-Continental Ballistic Missiles), which were favored over large advanced bomber aircraft as the Soviet Union's main pre-occupation in regards to development of strategic strike systems. The lack of extensive intelligence, misinterpretation of available intelligence and sometimes miss-direction by those vying for program funds, led to the United States unfounded fear that Soviet bomber developments in the early to late 1950's was more of a threat than it actually was.

It was expected that by the early 1960's the Soviets could field a Mach 2.0 plus bomber capable of operating at altitudes of 61,000 ft or greater. Such a bomber would be immune to interception by the Convair F-102 Deltas Dagger; the standard US interceptor in the late 1950's. For the timeframe beyond 1962 the performance projections for the Soviet bomber threat was estimated at between Mach 2.2 to 2.7 at altitudes up to 65,000 ft.

More or less in concert with the ongoing MX-1554 project, as early as 1953, research organizations were asked to look at the possibility of fielding an interceptor with cruise speeds up to Mach 4.05 to meet the projected post 1960's bomber threat. Such an aircraft would obviously have had to be very large, with a take-off weight of around 150,000 lb being estimated. It was clear, however, that such an aircraft was beyond the scope of then current or near term projected technology levels.

A further round of design studies commenced in 1955, this time for an interceptor with much reduced performance capabilities; cruise speed being put at Mach 1.17 at an altitude of around 60,000 ft, with a maximum combat speed, for short periods, of around Mach 2.5 at 63,000 ft. Such an aircraft could be smaller than the previous studies, with an estimated take-off weight of around 98,000 lb. While such a design was within the projected technological levels required for an aircraft for service in the early 1960's it fell short of the performance required to counter the projected bomber threat, which was put at up to Mach 2.7 speeds by 1963.

The new interceptor would be required to investigate DEW (Distant Early Warming) Line violations, and, if necessary, intercept threat aircraft. The DEW Line, which would become operational in 1957, was a chain of early warning radar stations in the far north of Canada, Alaska and Greenland. The aircraft was also to be capable of operating with or within the SAGE (Semi-Automatic Ground Environment), which correlated information from many air and ground systems which were coalesced to enhance the defense systems tactical picture.

Phase I of the advanced interceptor program for the USAF was concluded in September 1955, following which North American Aviation put its proposal forward in competition with designs from other manufacturers, including

Lockheed and Northrop, to meet GOR (General Operational Requirement) 114, which was formally issued on 6 October 1955. All of the designs, however, fell short of requirements. The USAF then apparently issued North American, Lockheed and Northrop contracts for studies into the required technologies for the advanced interceptor.

Despite none of the contractors meeting the program requirements North American Aviation received a Letter Contract on 7 June (some documentation states a date of 1 June) 1957 to build a two-crew, twin-engine all-weather long-range interceptor with a design speed of Mach 3.0 that would be capable of "swift maneuver" at altitudes up to 70,000 ft. The aircraft, referred to as Weapon System 202A, was to be armed with at least two air to air missiles, with either conventional or nuclear warheads, to be housed in an internal weapons bay. The power plant would be a variant of the General Electric J93 turbojet, which was itself being developed from the USAF's X-279E engine program.

Other contractors included the Hughes Aircraft Corporation, which was responsible for the fire-control system and the GAR-9 missile armament; Convair would build the wing; the Federal Division of the International Telephone & Telegraph Company was to provide the 'mission and traffic control system'; Electronic Specialty was to develop the antenna system; Hamilton Standard would provide the air conditioning and pressurization systems and Marquardt would provide the air induction control system.

In 1957, Hughes was selected to develop the GAR-X/YX-1 weapon and fire control system for the new interceptor. The YX-1 radar was designed with a large 40-in diameter antenna that would allow targets to be detected at ranges out to in excess of 100 nautical miles at all practical altitudes. The system was to be backed up by an unspecified infra-red search and track system. Although later development would lead to a missile with a range in excess of 100 miles, the GAR-X designed for the F-108 had a realistic range of between 15-25 miles, to engage targets which would be destroyed by either conventional or nuclear warheads, the latter consisting of a 0.28 kiloton W24 nuclear device. The maximum load of three GAR-X missiles would have been carried in an internal weapons bay as the F-108A's sole armament. During the development phase of the F-108 program the missile was re-designated GAR-9 and the fire control system was re-designated ASG-18. In 1962 the GAR-9 was re-designated the AIM-47, named 'Falcon', but this post dated the F-108A program.

North American Aviation had a wealth of experience in jet fighter design, including the F-86 Sabre and F-100 Super Sabre; the latter being the USAF's first supersonic fighter. At the time of the F-108A design, North American Aviation was also working on the large A3J (later RA-5C) Vigilante for the USN (United States Navy) and the much larger XB-70 Mach 3+ Strategic bomber; the latter aircraft would share some technologies and design practices with the F-108, including the honeycomb stainless steel materials, engines and similar designed crew escape capsule. Concurrently with the F-108 and XB-70 programs, North American was also developing the X-15 Rocket powered research aircraft which was delivered to NASA in 1959. The X-15's would eventually go on to set unofficial world speed and altitude records of Mach 6.7 (4,520 mph) and 354,000 ft respectively. The main aim of the program was to "investigate all aspects of piloted hypersonic flight".

Conceived in the late 1950's, the F-108 went through a number of design iterations leading up to and beyond the mock-up inspection in January 1959. In designing aircraft like the F-108A and the XB-70A the problem of "aerodynamic heating" associated with the very high speed surface friction, coupled with the radiant heat caused by the aircraft's powerful engines, had to be overcome. Much of what we know and infer about the F-108 design comes from the actual manufacturing work conducted later on the 2 XB-70A's. Of course, much more is known about the larger XB-70A, simply because this aircraft was built and flown. However, much can be learned of the F-108 by studying the XB-70. For example, the "(brazed) stainless steel honeycomb sandwich (panels) and titanium" martial of which the XB-70 was largely constructed would have been analogous to the F-108A, albeit with variations in manufacturing. The similarity stemmed from the fact that both aircraft were designed to cruise at high altitudes at speeds of Mach 3 and Mach 3+ that would generate very high surface temperatures, which at Mach 3 would range from between 400° to 600° Fahrenheit. Higher still was the 900° Fahrenheit heat that the framework around the J93 engines would have been subjected to.

Preventing overheating of the crew compartment at such high speeds also had to be accomplished. With the XB-70 this was done by development of a "transpiration" system employing bleed air which drove a pair of refrigeration pumps to provide the air to cool the aircraft cabin and equipment bays. A variation of this system would probably have been employed on the F-108A.

As with the larger XB-70 the F108A was designed with a crew escape capsule instead of the traditional ejection seat system. Very little is known about the F-108A crew escape capsule, but it can be assumed that the F-108A and XB-70A systems would have shared much commonality. Although there would have been obvious differences; one designed for an interceptor and the other for a large strategic bomber, it would be logical to assume that the F-108A capsule would have functioned in a similar fashion to that of the larger XB-70A capsule. The following manufacturers release from the early 1960's depicts the role and function of the B-70 crew escape capsule:

"The encapsulated ejection seat of the B-70 provides the crew members with secondary shirtsleeve environment in the event of a malfunction in the normal air vehicle system.

The crew members may encapsulate themselves within the escape capsule and continue to fly the air vehicle with limited capabilities. If a serious malfunction occurs that causes abandonment of the air vehicle, the crew members can eject themselves from the air vehicle. The escape capsule, with its clam shell doors closed and sealed, provides a safe environment for the crew members during ejection and descent to earth. Booms, which extend during the ejection process, provide aerodynamic stability, and a recovery parachute is automatically sequenced to open when a capsule descends to 15,000 feet. A pressurized bladder on the bottom of the capsule cushions the impact on touchdown."

In summary, the basic F-108A was to have a 15 minute turnaround capability, cruise and engage targets at Mach 3 with a roughly 1,000 nautical mile combat radius. The vehicle was to be capable of 1.2 g maneuvers at altitudes in excess of 77,000 ft and be capable of a zoom climb to 100,000 ft. When cruising at a combat altitude of 70,000 ft, the aircraft was to be capable of engaging any type of "air breathing vehicle" at altitudes ranging from 100,000 ft. down to sea level.

The Convair F-102A, developed under the MX-1554 program, was the first operational supersonic interceptor to enter service with the USAF. The MX-1554 program also led to the Convair F-106A/B, which was a stalwart of ADC for several decades during the Cold War. USAF

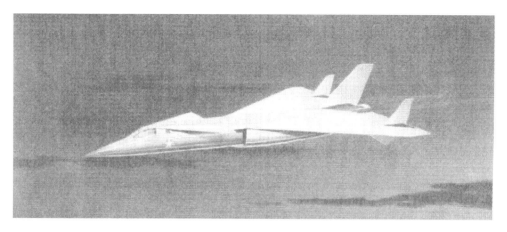

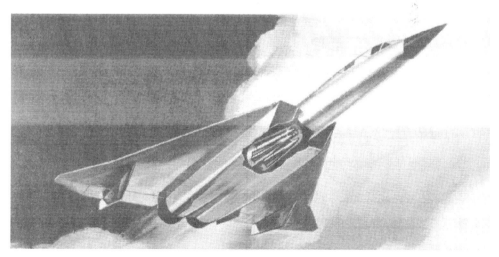

From top to bottom: Artist impressions of the three design iterations of the NA-257 from 1958 leading to the Mock-up inspection in January 1959. USAF

2

NORTH AMERICAN F-108A DESIGN ITERATIONS

The official mission description for the F-108A was given as "…the interception and destruction of hostile aircraft in-flight during day or night and in all weather". In 1957, the USAF was looking to fund 480 F-108A interceptors and hoped to get the aircraft into service with an initial operational capability in 1963.

First Design Iteration Dated 2 May 1958

The initial F-108A design emerged as a delta-winged aircraft featuring forward mounted canard surfaces, which like the "all-flying" canard surfaces on the XB-70A, would have had a primary function of balancing pitch (up/down) forces. The design also featured three vertical stabilizers, one of which was mounted on the rear fuselage centerline with the other two at the mid-point on the wing trailing edge, providing high-speed stabilization when flying at speeds in excess of Mach 2. The wings also featured elevons (the elevon is basically a combined elevator and aileron that is used for pitch and roll control in an aircraft).

Documentation dated 2 May 1958 (during the pre mock-up phase) showed the North American Model NA-257 – F-108A with a length of 84.9 ft; wingspan 52.9 ft; wing area 1400 sq. ft.; height 22.1 ft. and a tread of 10.4 ft. The aircraft was to be equipped with **speed brakes, nose wheel steering**, a pressurized fuel system; a nitrogen fuel system purging; liquid oxygen system; encapsulated crew seats; variable geometry inlet ducts and engine thrust reversers (for use in icy conditions). The only armament was 3 x GAR-9 missiles, with no provision for guns or offensive stores such as bombs.

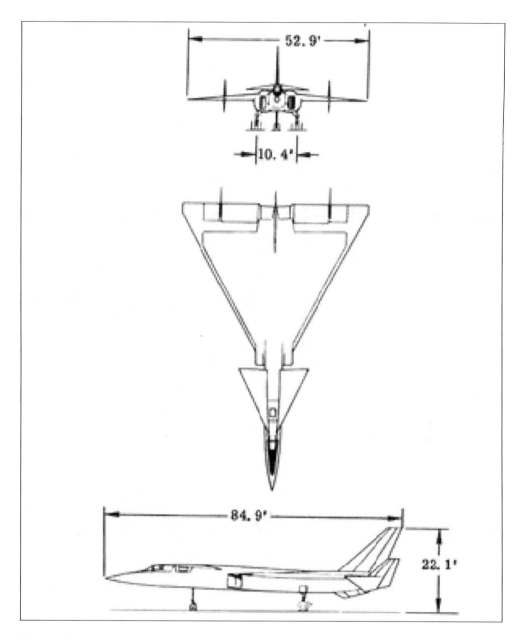

Three-view general arrangement drawing of the initial NA-257 design of summer 1958. USAF

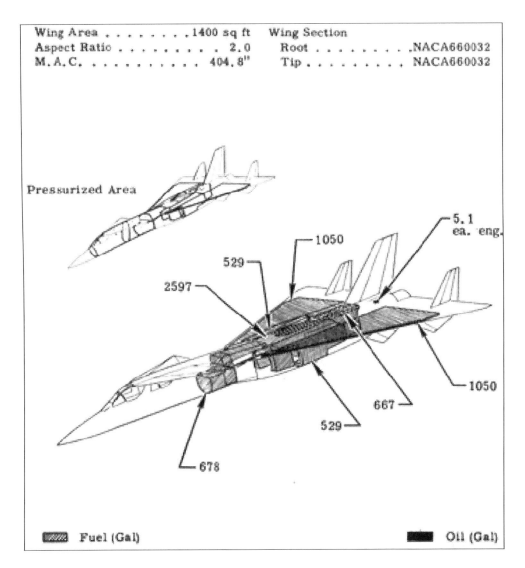

Wing Area . . . . .1400 sq ft   Wing Section
Aspect Ratio . . . . 2.0   Root NACA660032
M.A.C. . . . . 404.8"   Tip NACA660032

Pressurized Area

5.1 ea. eng.

1050

529

2597

1050

667

529

678

Fuel (Gal)   Oil (Gal)

Diagram showing the fuel and oil tank locations and capacity and the pressurization areas of the May 1958 Model NA-257. USAF

The maximum internal fuel capacity was set at 7100 Gal housed in the pressurized fuel system incorporating nitrogen purging, with seven fuel tanks; 2 in the wings and 5 in the fuselage. The wing tanks held a total of 2100 Gal and the fuselage tanks held 5000 Gal for a combined total of 7100 Gal of JP-6 fuel. Two oil tanks were located in the fuselage; these holding a combined total of 10.2 Gal of oil.

The aircraft's fire control system would provide "primary and auxiliary navigation, target search and detection and missile guidance in all-weather, all altitude operation against heavy enemy countermeasures, operating under SAGE or lesser ground control environment."

The electronics suite consisted of UHF Command, UHF Emergency, HF Command (voice plus digital), Intercom, BROFICON, Marker Beacon, Localizer, Glide Slope, UHF Data Link (receiver), TACAN, Identification Air-to-Air, Identification Air-to-Ground and Flare-out Altimeter.

Projected weights for the aircraft were 48,193 lb empty, 81,765 lb for a point interception mission, 73,369 lb for an area interception and 99,400 lb maximum take off; the latter limited by structure.

The aircraft would have required a ground run area of 3,100 ft and an area of 5,060 ft to reach an altitude of 50 ft. Maximum and combat speeds on a point interception mission profile were given as 1721 knots at maximum power at a maximum altitude of 73,600 ft. Basic speed at 50,000 ft was given as 1525 knots. On a point interception at operational take-off weight the aircraft was to have a 24,100 fpm (feet per minute) climb rate at maximum power, and be capable of a climb from sea level to 76,300 ft in 11.2 minutes at maximum power. Stalling speed on an area interception mission profile was given as 131.5 knots in power-off landing configuration, take-off weight.

On a typical point interception mission profile the aircraft was to be capable of taking off and climbing to an altitude of 76,300 feet, intercepting the target then loiter for 158.4 minutes at an altitude of 35,000 ft before returning to base in a mission time of 174.6 minutes. A typical area interception at a distance of 877 nautical miles and an average speed of 1721 knots was stipulated in a mission time of 1.25 hours. This would involve a take off and climb to 68,700 ft, followed by an interception of a target at 76,800 ft, descent to 75,600 ft and return to base.

F-108A Dimensions

2 May 1958

Wing
Span	52.9 ft
Incidence (root)	1°
(tip)	-4°
Dihedral	0°
Sweepback (25% chord)	53.5°
Length	84.9 ft
Height	22.1 ft
Tread	10.4 ft

Data taken from USAF 'Black Book' on F-108A

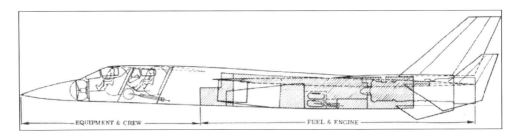

Diagram of the May 1958 Model NA-257 – F-108A showing the engine, fuel, equipment and crew compartments. USAF

Power Plant

Number and model	2 x J93-GE-1
Manufacturer	General Electric
Engine Spec Nr.	E-734
Type	Turbo Jet
Length	251 ft
Max Diameter	*52.5 ft
Weight (dry)	*4,875 lb
Jet Nozzle	Convergent Divergent
Augmentation	Afterburner

*With thrust reverser

Each of the 2 J93-GE-1 engines had the following ratings:

SLS	LB	RPM	MIN
Max	24,800	6625	*30
Mil	16,900	6625	Cont.
Nor	15,900	6625	Cont.

*Continuous afterburner power settings were available for supersonic cruise

Data taken from USAF 'Black Book' on F-108A

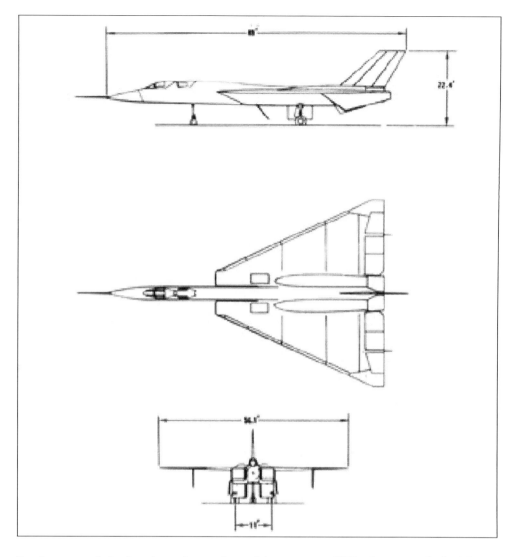

In the second design iteration, released in autumn 1958, the canards had been dropped, the aircraft taking on the appearance of a pure delta. USAF

Second Design Iteration Dated 1 October 1958

Emerging technology, design capability and changing operational requirements led to a number of changes to the design being implemented during the summer and autumn months of 1958, leading to a new design release of the NA-257 on 1 October that year as the program approached the mock-up phase. The most visible difference was the deletion of the large shoulder mounted forward canards of the earlier iteration. In addition, the upper sections of the three stabilizers were removed; the ventral sections remaining, and there were some changes to the shape of the engine intakes.

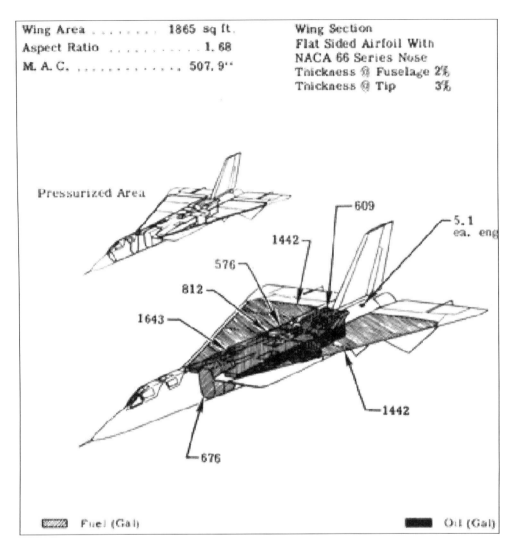

Wing Area . . . . 1865 sq ft.
Aspect Ratio 1. 68
M. A. C. . . . . 507. 9"

Wing Section
Flat Sided Airfoil With
NACA 66 Series Nose
Thickness @ Fuselage 2%
Thickness @ Tip   3%

Pressurized Area

609
5. 1 ea. eng
1442
576
812
1643
1442
676

Fuel (Gal)   Oil (Gal)

Diagram showing the fuel and oil tank locations and capacity and the pressurization areas of the October 1958 Model NA-257 - F-108A. USAF

The aircraft was redesigned to the following dimensions: length 89.0 ft.; wingspan 56.1 ft; wing area 1865 sq. ft; height 22.4 ft; aspect ratio 1.68 and M.A.C. 507.9". The engines had more or less the same settings as before with the exception that RPM had changed to 6650. Maximum internal fuel capacity was increased from 7100 to 7200 Gal. The new design had slightly higher weights than its predecessor; 49,796 lb empty, 82,485 lb combat weight for a point interception mission, 75,145 lb for an area interception mission and 101,800 lb. maximum take-off; limited by structure.

As with its predecessor the fuel was to be housed in a pressurized fuel system incorporating nitrogen purging, with seven fuel tanks; 2 in the wings and 5 in the fuselage. The wing tanks now held 2884 Gal and the fuselage tanks now held 4316 Gal for a combined total of 7200 Gal of JP-6 fuel. Oil tank capacity remained the same as before.

The fire control system and electronics suite remained more or less the same, but there was no mention in the new specification of the Flare-out Altimeter. The cockpit would be designed with "air conditioning, liquid oxygen, pressurization, encapsulated seats and an automatic flight control system".

The new specification called for a reduced take-off run area of 2,880 ft instead of the 3,100 ft required for the earlier iteration. An altitude of 50 ft was to be attained in 4,750 ft, which was 300 ft shorter than the 5,050 ft stipulated for the earlier integration. Maximum and combat speeds on a point interception were given as 1721 knots at maximum power at a maximum altitude of 77,000 ft and 73,400 ft respectively. Basic speed at 50,000 ft was given as 1526 knots - 1 knot higher that before. On a point interception at operational take-off weight the aircraft was to have a 25,100 fpm climb rate at maximum power at sea level, increasing to 30,400 fpm at combat weight at sea level. On a point interception configuration the aircraft was to climb from sea level to 77,000 ft in 11.5 minutes at take-off weight and maximum power. Stalling speed on an area interception profile was given as 119 knots in power-off landing configuration, take-off weight; 12 knots lower than the earlier iteration. Ceiling on a point intercept configuration was 73,350 ft. at 100 fpm at take-off weight at maximum power. Ferry range was stipulated as 2,281 nautical miles with the 7200 Gal internal fuel at an average speed of 553 knots for a duration of 4.12 hours at a take-off weight of 99,640 lb.

Naturally, with the new design the data for various mission profiles was altered: For a typical point interception mission profile the aircraft would take off and climb to an altitude of 77,000 ft., intercept the target then descend to 35,000 ft where it was to be capable of loitering for 176 minutes before returning to base. This would require a mission time of 192.5 minutes. A typical area interception at a distance of 883 nautical miles and an average speed of 1721 knots was stipulated in a mission time of 1.26 hours. This would involve a take off and climb to an altitude of 69,000 ft. followed by an interception of a target at 78,950 ft, then a descent to 76,000 ft and return to base.

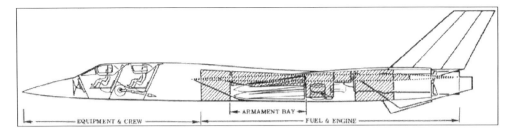

Diagram of the October 1958 NA-257 - F-108A iteration showing the engine, fuel, equipment and crew compartments. USAF

F-108A Dimensions

1 October 1958

Wing
Span	56.1 ft
Incidence (root)	0°
(tip)	0°
Dihedral	0°
Sweepback (25% chord)	58.0°
Length	89.0 ft
Height	22.4 ft
Tread	11.0 ft

Power Plant

Number and model	2 x J93-GE-1
Manufacturer	General Electric
Engine Spec Nr.	E-734
Type	Turbo Jet
Length	233.8 ft
Max Diameter	*56.0 ft
Weight (dry)	*4,874 lb
Jet Nozzle	Convergent Divergent
Augmentation	Afterburner

*With thrust reverser

Data taken from USAF 'Black Book' on F-108A

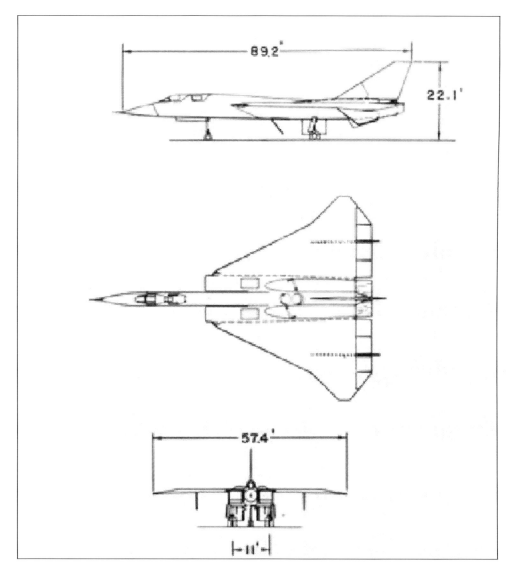

In the third design iteration, released in December 1958, the aircrafts wings and overall dimensions were further altered; the wing featuring downward droop at the outer sections. USAF

15 December 1958 Design, final revision for the January 1959 Mock-Up

As the design team pushed towards the mock-up configuration a new design iteration of the NA-257 was released on 15 December 1958. The electronics suite remained the same, but there were many internal and external changes. The most visible difference was the re-designed cranked-delta wing with anhedral at the tips. The new wing, effectively a double-delta design, had a 65° sweep and the winglets were designed with a droop and a 45° sweep. Length was slightly increased to 89.2 ft; wingspan increased to 57.4 ft; wing area remained at 1965 sq. ft. and height was slightly reduced to 22.1 ft. A new variant of the engine designated J93-GE-3R was specified; each of the two engines having the following ratings:

SLS	LB	RPM	MIN
Max	27,200	6825	Cont
Mil	18,500	6825	Cont.
Nor	17,500	6825	Cont.

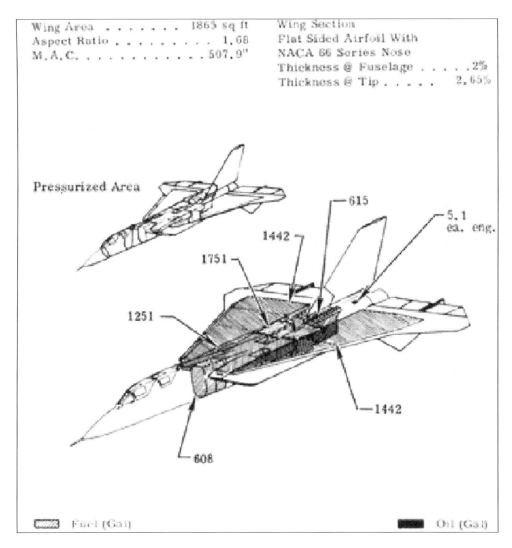

Fuel and oil tank locations and capacity and the pressurization areas of the winter 1958 Model NA-257 - F-108A. USAF

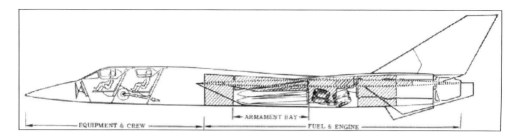

ARMAMENT BAY

EQUIPMENT & CREW   FUEL & ENGINE

Diagram of the design iteration of the NA-257 (F-108A) released in December 1958, showing the engine, fuel, equipment and crew compartments. USAF

Maximum internal fuel capacity was reduced from 7200 to 7109 gal, now housed in only 6 fuel tanks; 2 in the wings and 4 in the fuselage. The wing tanks held a total of 2884 Gal and the fuselage tanks now held 4225 Gal for a combined total of 7109 Gal of JP-6 fuel.

The new design had higher weights than its predecessors, 50,544 lb empty; 50,908 lb basic; 74,084 lb design and 85,327 lb at combat weight for a point interception mission; 75,719 lb for an area interception (basic mission) and 102,234 lb maximum take off; 96,719 lb max loading; limited by structure.

The new specification called for a reduced take-off run area of 2,800 ft instead of the 2,880 ft required for the earlier iteration. An altitude of 50 ft was to be reached in 4,510 ft, which was 240 ft shorter than the 4,750 ft of the earlier design and 540 ft shorter than the 5,050 ft stipulated for the May 1958 design. Maximum and combat speeds on a point interception were given as 1721 knots at maximum power at a maximum altitude of 76,600 ft and 74,100 ft respectively. Basic speed at 50,000 ft remained the same at 1526 knots. On a point interception at operational take-off weight the aircraft was to have a 25,750 fpm climb at maximum power at sea level, increasing to 35,500 fpm at combat weight at sea level. These figures were higher than the 25,100 and 30,400 fpm respectively for the October 1958 design. On a point interception configuration the aircraft was to be capable of climbing from sea level to 77,600 ft in 9.4 minutes at take-off weight and maximum power; a significant improvement on the climb to 77,000 ft in 11.5 minutes stipulated in the earlier design. Stalling speed on an area interception profile was given as 128 knots in power-off landing configuration, take-off weight; 9 knots higher than the earlier iteration, being closer to the 131 knots of the May 1958 design. Ceiling on a point interception configuration was now 74,000 ft at 100 fpm at take-off weight and maximum power. The slightly reduced ferry range was stipulated as 2,184 nautical miles with the 7109 Gal internal fuel at a slightly reduced average speed of 550 knots for a flight duration of 4.01 hours at a take-off weight of 99,780 lb.

Data for various mission profiles was altered: For a typical point interception mission the aircraft would take off and climb to 77,600 ft, intercept the target then descend to 35,000 ft. where it was to be capable of loitering for 186 minutes before returning to base. This would require a mission time of 200.4 minutes. A typical area interception mission at a distance of 887 nautical miles at an average speed of 1721 knots was stipulated in a mission time of 1.24 hours. This would involve a take off and climb to 69,100 ft followed by an interception of a target at 80,000 ft, then a descent to 76,200 ft and then return to base.

F-108A Dimensions

15 December 1958

Wing

Span	57.4 ft.
Incidence (root)	0°
(tip)	-3°
Dihedral	0°
Sweepback (25% chord)	
Inboard	58.1°
Outboard	32.1°
Length	89.2 ft.
Height	22.1 ft.
Tread	11.0 ft.

Power Plant

Number and model	2 x J93-GE-3R
Manufacturer	General Electric
Engine Spec Nr.	R58AGT288C
	Supplement A
Type	Axial Turbo Jet
Length	233.0 ft
Max Diameter	*59.0 ft
Weight (dry)	*5,115 lb
Tailpipe	Mech, Variable C/D (Convergent Divergent)
Augmentation	Afterburner
*With thrust reverser	

Data taken from USAF 'Black Book' on F-108A

Top: The Mock-up of the NA-257 - F-108A apparently under construction in late 1958. Above: The mock-up shown with twin-canopy covers and equipment bay doors open in early January 1959. USAF

Dummy GAR-9 missiles are shown in the fuselage internal weapons bay of the F-108A mock-up in mid-January 1959 as the program approached the mock-up inspection phase. The GAR-9, the planned F-108A's sole intended armament, was designed to be armed with either conventional or nuclear warheads. USAF

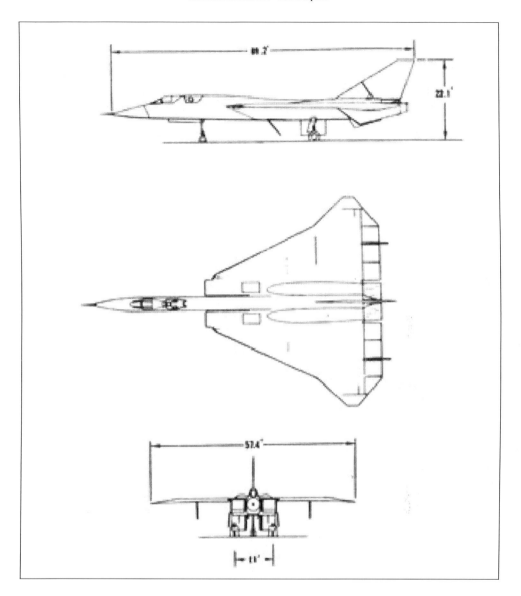

In the final iteration of the NA-257 - F-108, which emerged post mock-up inspection, the aircraft retained the basic layout and dimensions as before, the main changes being internal. USAF

Final Design Iteration before Cancellation

An inspection of the mock-up on 26 January 1959 resulted in a number of changes being put forward for the Model NA-257 - F-108, which was named 'Rapier' on 15 May that year. The changes resulted in the final design iteration before the project was cancelled being was released on 12 June 1959. The overall dimensions of the aircraft remained unchanged from the December

1958 design and the fire control system and electronics suite remained the same. However, a new more powerful variant of the J93 engine was incorporated; each of these engines, designated J93-GE-3AR, having the following ratings:

SLS	LB	RPM	MIM
Max	29,300	6825	Cont.
Mil	20,900	6825	Cont.
Nor	18,400	6825	Cont

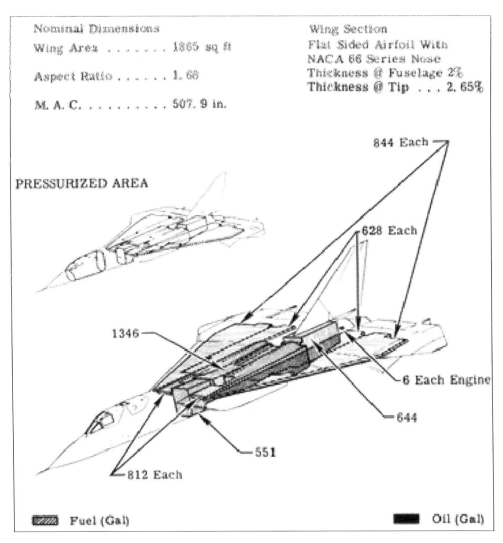

Nominal Dimensions

Wing Area . . . . 1865 sq ft

Aspect Ratio 1.68

M. A. C. . . . . 507.9 in.

Wing Section

Flat Sided Airfoil With NACA 66 Series Nose
Thickness @ Fuselage 2%
Thickness @ Tip . . . 2.65%

PRESSURIZED AREA

844 Each

628 Each

1346

6 Each Engine

644

551

812 Each

Fuel (Gal)   Oil (Gal)

Fuel and oil tank locations and capacity and pressurization areas of the final iteration of the NA-257 - F-108 post mock-up inspection. USAF

The basic description for the final design iteration would be a twin-engine, 2 crew low-aspect-ratio delta-wing (cranked-delta) aircraft featuring an all-moving vertical stabilizer, fixed ventral, elevons, employed for pitch and roll control, nose-wheel steering, speed brakes, variable-geometry engine inlets, reverse thrust capability with an internal weapons bay for three large GAR-9 air to air missiles. The crew would be contained in a pressurized compartment allowing operations to be conducted in a "shirt sleeve environment". Among the cockpit instrumentation was a "complete attack system".

Internal fuel capacity remained unchanged at 7109 Gal, but the number of fuel tanks was increased to nine; 4 in the wings and 5 in the fuselage. The wing tanks held a total of 2944 Gal while the fuselage tanks held a total of 4165 Gal, for a combined wing and fuselage total of 7109 Gal. Oil capacity was also increased; the two oil tanks located in the fuselage now housing 12.0 Gal instead of the 10.2 Gal of the previous designs.

At 50,907 lb the basic empty weight was higher than its predecessors. Combat weight was put at 86,253 lb on a point interception mission and 76,118 lb on an area interception; both figures being slightly higher than the previous design weights. Maximum take of weight was also slightly higher at 102,533 lb., limited by structure.

The unassisted take-off run was reduced from 2,800 ft to 2,660 ft, and an altitude of 50 ft was to be attained in 4,275 ft, which was 235 ft shorter than the 4,510 ft of the earlier design and 775 ft shorter than the 5,050 ft stipulated for the May 1958 design. Maximum and combat speeds on a point interception mission were given as 1721 knots at maximum power at a maximum altitude of 77,400 ft and 73,900 ft respectively. Basic speed at 50,000 ft remained the same at 1526 knots.

The more powerful engines improved the aircrafts planned climb performance which now called for a climb rate of 32,600 fpm at sea level on a point interception at operational take-off weight, increasing to 39,600 fpm at combat weight at sea level. These figures were a significant increase on the 25,750 fpm and 35,500 fpm respectively of the December 1958 design iteration. On a point interception configuration the aircraft was to be capable of climbing from sea level to 77,400 ft in 8.4 minutes at take-off weight and maximum power. The aircraft's projected stalling speed on an area interception profile remained the same as before at 128 knots in power-off landing configuration, take-off weight. Ceiling on a point interception configuration was now 73,950 ft at 100 fpm at take-off weight at maximum power and 77,400 ft at 500 fpm at combat weight and maximum power. The aircraft's ferry range was reduced from 2,184 nautical miles to 2,161 nautical miles with the 7109 Gal internal fuel at an average speed of 550 knots for a flight duration of 3.92 hours at a take-off weight of 100,094 lb.

The change in power and weight levels of the aircraft resulted in another change in mission profiles figures. The new figures for a typical point interception mission profile would have the aircraft take off and climb to 77,400 ft, intercept the target, then descend to 35,000 ft where it was to be capable of loitering for 180 minutes before returning to base in a mission duration of 193.6 minutes; a 6.8 minute reduction in mission endurance. A typical area interception at a distance of 887 nautical miles and an average speed of 1721 knots was stipulated in the slightly reduced mission time of 1.20 hours. This would involve a take off and climb to 69,000 ft followed by an interception of a target at 79.400 ft, then a descent to 76,000 ft and then return to base.

Dimensions F-108A 12 June 1959

Wing

Span	57.4 ft.
Incidence (root)	0°
(tip)	-3°
Dihedral	0°
Sweepback (25% chord)	
Inboard	58.1°
Outboard	32.1°
Length	89.2 ft.
Height	22.1 ft.
Tread	11.0 ft.

Power Plant

Number and model	2 x J93-GE-3AR
Manufacturer	General Electric
Engine Spec Nr.	R58AGT288E
	Supplement A
Type	Axial Turbo Jet
Length	233.0 ft
Max Diameter	*59.0 ft
Weight (dry)	*5,115 lb
Tailpipe	Mech, Variable C/D (Convergent Divergent)
Augmentation	Afterburner
*With thrust reverser	

Note 1: The Mock up, it has been claimed, was inspected by the USAF on 20 January 1959. However, the Mock-up inspection date is stated in official documentation as being 26 January 1959.

Note 2: The design release dates given are the dates given on the Standard USAF 'Black Book' Characteristics Documents, which would have been prepared after the finalization of each design point.

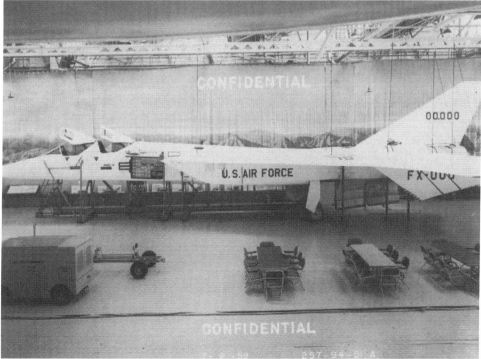

Two views of the mock-up on 7 February 1959. USAF

Top: The mock-up nose section showing the ASG-18 long-range pulse-Doppler look-up/look down radar fire control system. Above: The GAR-9 missile. USAF

Previous page top: The mock-up shown on 27 July 1959, a few months before
the program was cancelled. Previous page bottom: The F-108A would have been
powered by a variant of the powerful General Electric J93 turbojet engine, which
went on to power the two North American XB-70A's. Above: The XB-70A
Valkyrie escape capsule during a test drop. Although there would have been
differences such as in size, the F-108A escape capsule may have been expected
to operate in a similar fashion. USAF

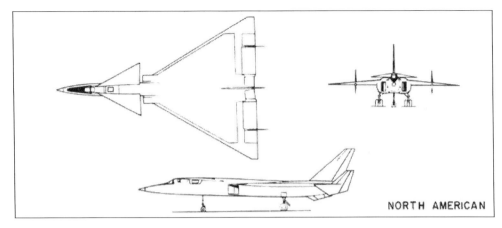

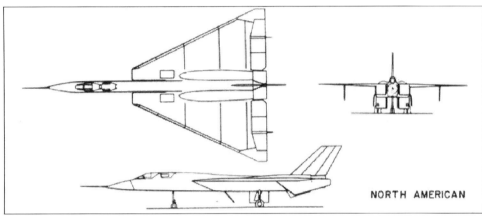

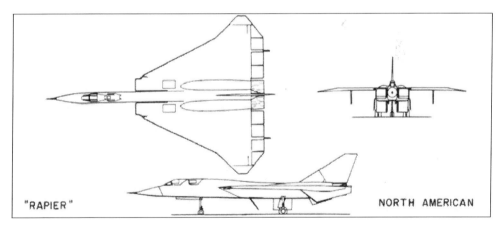

The three main configurations of the NA-257 - F-108A from summer 1958 (top), autumn 1958 (centre) and June 1959 (bottom). The June 1959 configuration was more or less identical externally to the mock-up configuration of December 1958. USAF

3

POSTSCRIPT

The XF-108, like its larger sister, the XB-70 strategic bomber, was a very ambitious program. However, unlike the XB-70 the XF-108 never flew; the program being cancelled on 23 September 1959 while at the mock-up stage, at which point some $141.9 million had been spent on research and development. Although there are many facts, fiction and theories for the aircraft's cancellation, the fact that ICBM's were set to take on the mantle of the main delivery vehicle for the Soviet Union's strategic nuclear weapons effectively rendered the aircraft redundant in its intended role; the advanced Soviet bombers not materializing as both Superpowers increasingly moved towards ICBM's, which were favored over vulnerable manned bombers. Prior to its cancellation the estimated first flight date for the F-108 was March 1961, although, had the program continued it would probably have encountered delays as evidenced by the delays encountered by the XB-70A program.

The XB-70A program was also cancelled a few years later, but two aircraft were built and flown as research aircraft. XB-70A No.1 (S/N: 62-001) conducted its maiden flight on 21 September 1964, followed by XB-70A No.2 (S/N: 62-207) on 17 July 1965. Aircraft No.1, which achieved Mach 3 flight on 14 October 1965, flew on research flights with the USAF and later NASA; being retired to the National Museum of the USAF at Wright Patterson Air Force Base, Ohio, where it was flown to on its 83rd and final flight on 4 February 1969. Twenty five of the 83 flights were flown on NASA test flights, the first of these taking place on 25 April 1967. The No.2 XB-70A was lost when it crashed on its 46th flight following a mid-air collision with a NASA Lockheed F-104A chase aircraft on 8 June 1966.

Although the F-108 was destined never to fly elements of the program were carried over to the 1960's Lockheed YF-12A Mach 3+ interceptor program, including the powerful ASG-18 long-range look-up/look down pulse-Doppler radar fire control system and the AIM-47 (GAR-9) missile; three of which would have been carried in the F-108A's internal weapons bay as the sole armament. Like the F-108A, the planned F-12 interceptor, developed from the Lockheed A-12, was a large aircraft capable of containing the huge powerful radar with its 40-in diameter antenna dish housed in the aircraft nose. As well as being fitted to an YF-12, the radar system was extensively tested in a Convair B-58 Hustler supersonic strategic bomber, which had a modified dropping nose, earning it the nickname 'Snoopy'. The radar fire control system was to be integrated with the AIM-47 long-range radar guided air to air missile, which was to have been armed with either conventional or nuclear warheads had it gone into service.

With the cancellation of the F-108 program the USAF was left with less capable interceptors like the Convair F-106 to counter the reducing threat of Soviet bombers. This F-106A has just launched an AIR-2A Genie air to air rocket, which in its operational form was armed with a nuclear warhead. USAF

The first un-powered separation drop test of an AIM-47 was conducted on 16 April 1964 and the first powered launch of the missile took place on 18 March 1965. There were seven powered launches at various speeds and altitudes up to Mach 3.2 and 75,000-ft. The missile tests were considered to have been partially successful, although the system was never tested in an operational environment, effectively being cancelled when the F-12 program was cancelled in 1968, although it would form the basis for development of the Hughes AIM-54 Phoenix long-range air to air missile developed for the cancelled Grumman F-111B naval fighter and its successor, the Grumman F-14 Tomcat; entering service on the latter aircraft.

For ADC, the potential interception of Soviet bombers and other potential introducers into CONUS (Continental United States) airspace would be undertaken by the McDonnell F-101B Voodoo and the Convair F-106 Delta Dart armed with the AIR-2A Genie nuclear armed air to air rocket and AIM-4 Falcon air to air missiles. The F-101B entered service with the USAF ADC 60th FIS at Otis AFB, Massachusetts on 5 January 1959, going on to serve with 17 ADC squadrons. Seven ANG squadrons were equipped with F-101B/F's, the first from November 1969, the Voodoo being retired from the interception role with the ANG in 1981.

The first F-106A development aircraft conducted its maiden flight on 26 December 1956, some eight months after the F-102A had entered operational service with ADC. The USAF received the first of 277 F-106A's in July 1959; 63 two-seat F-106B's were also delivered. The aircraft became operational with the 498th FIS at Geiger AFB, Washington, in October 1959 and was retired from ANG service in August 1988.

While the F-108 was never built and flown the North American Aviation stables much larger XB-70, two of which were built, flew 129 times between 1964 and 1969. US DoD

Another Mach 3 interceptor, the Lockheed F-12, was developed for the USAF, this too falling by the wayside in 1968. Top: YF-12 S/N: 60-6935 lifts off on a development flight. Above: The F-12 would have been armed with a developed variant of the GAR-9, known as the AIM-47. USAF

APPENDICES

APPENDIX I

LOADING AND PERFORMANCE CHART FOR THE NORTH AMERICAN MODEL NA-257 – F-108A DATED 2 MAY 1958

Loading and Performance — Typical Mission

CONDITIONS			INTERCEPTOR MISSIONS					FERRY RANGE
			BASIC		DESIGN	ALTERNATE		
			AREA	POINT		DASH	LOITER	
			I	II	III	IV	V	VI
TAKE-OFF WEIGHT		(lb)	99,400	99,400	99,400	80,171	89,400	97,240
Fuel at 6.7 lb/gal (grade JP-6)		(lb)	47,570	47,570	47,570	28,341	47,570	47,570
Payload (missile)		(lb)	2160	2160	2160	2160	2160	none
Wing loading		(psf)	71.0	71.0	71.0	57.3	71.0	69.6
Stall speed (power off)		(kn)	131.5	131.5	131.5	118.5	131.5	130.0
Take-off ground roll at SL		(ft)	3100	3100	3100	2020	3100	2980
Take-off to clear 50 ft		(ft)	5060	5060	5060	3420	5060	4860
Rate of climb at SL		(fpm)	24,100	24,100	24,100	30,250	24,100	24,700
Time: SL to 40,000 ft		(min)	6.2	6.2	6.2	4.9	6.2	6.0
Time: SL to 50,000 ft		(min)	7.1	7.1	7.1	5.6	7.1	6.9
Service ceiling (100 fpm)		(ft)	72,550	72,550	72,550	76,930	72,550	72,950
COMBAT RANGE		(n mi)						1984
COMBAT RADIUS		(n mi)	877		1002	350	604	
Average speed		(kn)	1721		1721	1721	1210	559
Initial cruising altitude		(ft)	68,700		68,700	73,100	36,152	33,200
Final cruising altitude		(ft)	75,400		75,700	76,000	75,700	45,400
Total mission time		(hr)	1.25		1.49	.70	2.71	3.61
TOTAL MISSION TIME		(hr)		2.91				
Interception altitude		(ft)		76,300				
COMBAT WEIGHT		(lb)	73,368	81,765	71,665	63,381	67,968	55,809
Combat altitude		(ft)	78,600	76,380	71,800	74,008	72,806	45,400
Combat speed		(kn)	1721	1721	1721	1721	1721	1415
Combat climb		(fpm)	500	500	13,400	13,800	13,550	63,500
Combat ceiling (500 fpm)		(ft)	78,600	76,380				83,700
Combat ceiling (1.2g)		(ft)			75,600	76,200	76,700	
Service ceiling (100 fpm)		(ft)	78,850	76,550	79,350	81,900	80,400	84,000
Max rate of climb at SL		(fpm)	33,250	33,700	34,000	38,700	36,000	44,000
Max speed at optimum altitude		(kn/ft)	1721/75,100	1721/73,800	1721/76,600	1721/74,900	1721/76,700	1721/80,700
Basic speed at 50,000 ft		(kn)	1525	1525	1525	1525	1525	1525
LANDING WEIGHT		(lb)	56,059	55,580	56,109	55,127	56,109	55,809
Ground roll at SL		(ft)	1900	1800	1820	1798	1820	1810
Total from 50 ft		(ft)	3200	3075	3100	3050	3100	3080

NOTES
1 Maximum power
2 Military power
3 Detailed descriptions of RADIUS and RANGE missions given on page 6
4 Allows for weight reduction during ground operations and climb
5 Allows 0.8 min for take-off and acceleration to best climb speed
6 Allows 1.2 min for take-off and acceleration to best climb speed
7 With 40% military thrust reverser

PERFORMANCE BASIS
(a) Data source: Estimated
(b) Performance is based on powers shown on page 6.

APPENDIX II

LOADING AND PERFORMANCE CHART FOR THE NORTH AMERICAN MODEL NA-257 – F-108A DATED 1 OCTOBER 1958

PRE-MOCKUP   S E C R E T

Loading and Performance — Typical Mission

CONDITIONS		INTERCEPTOR MISSIONS					FERRY RANGE
		BASIC		ALTERNATE			
		AREA	POINT	DESIGN	DASH	LOITER	
		I	II	III	IV	V	VI
TAKE-OFF WEIGHT	(lb)	101,800	101,800	101,800	83,048	101,800	99,640
Fuel at 6.7 lb/gal (grade JP-6)	(lb)	48,420	48,240	48,240	29,480	48,240	48,240
Payload (missiles)	(lb)	2160	2160	2160	2160	2160	None
Wing loading	(psf)	54.6	54.6	54.6	44.3	54.6	53.4
Stall speed (power off)	(kn)	119.0	119.0	119.0	107.6	119.0	117.7
Take-off ground roll at SL	(ft)	2880	2880	2880	1950	2980	2758
Take-off to clear 50 ft	(ft)	4750	4750	4750	3230	4750	4550
Rate of climb at SL	(fpm)	25,130	25,100	25,100	31,100	25,100	25,600
Time: SL to 40,000 ft	(min)	6.7	6.7	6.7	5.2	6.7	6.6
Time: SL to 50,000 ft	(min)	7.6	7.6	7.6	5.8	7.6	7.5
Service ceiling (100 fpm)	(ft)	73,350	73,350	73,350	77,800	73,350	73,850
COMBAT RANGE	(n mi)	----	----	----	----	----	2281
COMBAT RADIUS	(n mi)	883	----	1005	350	657	----
Average speed	(kn)	1721	----	1721	1721	1260	553
Initial cruising altitude	(ft)	69,200	----	69,200	73,500	36,152	45,900
Final cruising altitude	(ft)	76,000	----	76,300	76,350	76,000	45,800
Total mission time	(hr)	1.25	----	1.48	0.705	2.38	4.32
TOTAL MISSION TIME	(hr)	----	3.21	----	----	----	----
Interception altitude	(ft)	----	77,000	----	----	----	----
COMBAT WEIGHT	(lb)	75,345	82,485	73,436	64,920	70,405	57,162
Combat altitude	(ft)	76,950	77,000	72,200	74,466	72,900	45,900
Combat speed	(kn)	1721	1721	1721	1721	1721	1440
Combat climb	(fpm)	500	500	11,800	12,500	12,200	68,600
Combat ceiling (500 fpm)	(ft)	28,950	77,000	----	----	----	84,300
Combat ceiling (1.2g)	(ft)	----	----	75,800	78,400	76,650	----
Service ceiling (100 fpm)	(ft)	79,200	77,300	79,700	82,200	80,300	84,600
Max rate of climb at SL	(fpm)	33,400	30,400	34,300	39,300	35,900	44,900
Max speed at optimum altitude	(kn/ft)	1721/75,300	1721/73,400	1721/73,900	1721/75,400	1721/76,650	1721/81,600
Basic speed at 30,000 ft	(kn)	1526	1526	1526	1526	1526	1526
LANDING WEIGHT	(lb)	59,462	56,878	57,702	56,749	57,702	57,162
Ground roll at SL	(ft)	1880	1790	1820	1790	1820	1800
Total from 50 ft	(ft)	3175	3060	3100	3060	3100	3070

NOTES
① Maximum power
② Military power
③ Detailed descriptions of RADIUS and RANGE missions given on page 6
④ Allows for weight reduction during ground operations and climb
⑤ Allows 0.8 min for take-off and acceleration to best climb speed
⑥ Allows 1.2 min for take-off and acceleration to best climb speed
⑦ With 40% military thrust reverser

PERFORMANCE BASIS:
(a) Data source: Estimated data
(b) Performance is based on powers shown on page 6.

F-108A   S E C R E T   1 OCT 58

APPENDIX III

LOADING AND PERFORMANCE CHART FOR THE NORTH AMERICAN MODEL NA-257 – F-108A DATED 15 DECEMBER 1958

Loading and Performance — Typical Mission

CONDITIONS		INTERCEPTOR MISSIONS					FERRY RANGE
		BASIC		ALTERNATE			
		AREA I	POINT II	DESIGN III	DASH IV	LOITER V	VI
TAKE-OFF WEIGHT	(lb)	102,734	102,234	102,234	82,373	102,234	99,786
Fuel at 6.7 lb/gal (grade JP-6)	(lb)	47,632	47,632	47,632	27,771	47,632	47,632
Payload (missiles)	(lb)	2454	2454	2454	2454	2454	None
Wing loading	(psf)	54.9	54.9	54.9	44.1	54.9	53.5
Stall speed (power off)	(kn)	128.0	128.0	128.0	115.5	128.0	126.5
Take-off ground roll at SL ①	(ft)	2800	2800	2800	1760	2800	2630
Take-off to clear 50 ft ①	(ft)	4510	4510	4510	3080	4510	4280
Rate of climb at SL ①⑧	(fpm)	29,750	29,750	29,750	31,500	29,750	30,500
Rate of climb at SL (one eng out) ①⑧	(fpm)	5150	5150	5150	6830	5150	5320
Time: SL to 40,000 ft ①④	(min)	5.1 ⑥	5.1 ⑥	5.1 ⑥	3.9 ⑤	5.1 ⑥	4.3 ⑥
Time: SL to 50,000 ft ①④	(min)	5.9 ⑧	5.9 ⑧	5.9 ⑧	4.5 ⑤	5.9 ⑧	5.7 ⑧
Service ceiling (100 fpm)	(ft)	74,000	74,000	74,000	78,500	74,000	74,300
Service ceiling (one eng out)	(ft)	33,900	33,900	33,900	39,900	33,900	34,600
COMBAT RANGE ③	(n mi)	———	———	———	———	———	2184
COMBAT RADIUS ③	(n mi)	887	———	1009	330	640	———
Average speed	(kn)	1721	———	1721	1721	1200	550
Initial cruising altitude	(ft)	69,100	———	69,100	73,800	72,200	38,100
Final cruising altitude	(ft)	76,200	———	76,200	76,500	76,200	46,600
Total mission time	(hr)	1.24	———	1.46	.89	2.35	4.01
TOTAL MISSION TIME ④	(hr)	———	3.34	———	———	———	———
Interception altitude	(ft)	———	77,600	———	———	———	———
COMBAT WEIGHT	(lb)	75,719	85,327	74,084	65,801	70,869	57,850
Combat altitude ①	(ft)	80,000 ①	77,600 ①	72,500 ①	74,700 ①	73,400 ①	46,600 ②
Combat speed ①	(kn)	1721	1721	1721	1721	1721	1455
Combat climb ①	(fpm)	500	500	14,450	14,800	14,800	74,500
Combat ceiling (500 fpm)	(ft)	80,680	77,600	80,400	82,600	81,200	84,700
Combat ceiling (1.2g)	(ft)	76,600	74,100	77,000	79,450	77,900	81,800
Service ceiling (100 fpm)	(ft)	80,150	77,800	80,550	82,750	81,400	84,800
Service ceiling (one engine out)	(ft)	40,700	38,250	41,150	43,400	42,000	45,700
Max rate of climb at SL ①⑧	(fpm)	40,600	35,500	41,000	46,500	43,000	53,000
Time: 36,152 ft & 94M to 70,000 ft & 3.0M ①	(min)	4.3	5.1	4.2	3.7	4.0	3.7
Max speed at optimum altitude ①	(kn/ft)	1721/76,600	1721/74,100	1721/77,900	1721/79,450	1721/77,900	1721/81,800
Basic speed at 50,000 ft ①	(kn)	1526	1526	1526	1526	1526	1526
LANDING WEIGHT	(lb)	60,484	58,022	58,715	57,711	58,715	57,958
Ground roll at SL ⑦	(ft)	2010	1930	1950	1930	1950	1930
Total from 50 ft ⑦	(ft)	3330	3215	3245	3200	3245	3215
Touchdown speed	(kn)	132.0	130.6	130.5	129.5	130.5	130.0
Stall speed	(kn)	92.5	90.5	91.0	90.0	91.0	90.5
Wing loading	(psf)	32.4	31.1	31.5	31.0	31.5	31.1

NOTES

① Maximum power
② Military power
③ Detailed descriptions of RADIUS and RANGE missions given on page 6.
④ Allows for weight reduction during ground operations and climb

⑤ Allows 0.8 min for take-off and acceleration to best climb speed
⑥ Allows 1.2 min for take-off and acceleration to best climb speed

⑦ With 36.5% military thrust reverser
⑧ Instantaneous values

PERFORMANCE BASIS:
(a) Data source: Estimated
(b) Performance is based on powers shown on page 6

APPENDIX IV

LOADING AND PERFORMANCE CHART FOR THE NORTH AMERICAN MODEL NA-257 – F-108A DATED 12 JUNE 1959

MOCKUP   S E C R E T

Loading and Performance — Typical Mission

CONDITIONS		INTERCEPT MISSIONS					FERRY MISSION
		BASIC		ALTERNATE			
		AREA I	POINT II	DESIGN III	DASH IV	LOITER V	VI
TAKE-OFF WEIGHT (lb)		102,533	102,533	102,533	82,256	102,533	109,094
Fuel at 6.7 lb/gal (grade JP-6) (lb)		47,632	47,632	47,632	27,348	47,632	47,632
Payload (missiles) (lb)		2439	2439	2439	2439	2439	None
Wing loading (psf)		55.0	55.0	55.0	44.1	55.0	53.8
Stall speed (power off) (kn)		128	128	128	115	128	127
Take-off ground roll at SL (ft)	①	2660	2660	2660	1660	2660	2630
Take-off to clear 50 ft (ft)	①	4275	4275	4275	2030	4275	4080
Rate of climb at SL (fpm)	①	32,600	32,600	32,600	40,800	32,600	33,500
Rate of climb at SL (one eng out) (fpm)	①	6090	6090	6090	9080	6090	6280
Time: SL to 40,000 ft (min)	①④	4.6	4.6	4.6	3.5	4.6	4.5
Time: SL to 50,000 ft (min)	①④	5.4	5.4	5.4	4.1	5.4	5.2
Service ceiling (100 fpm) (ft)	①	73,950	73,950	73,950	78,550	73,950	74,450
Service ceiling (one engine out) (ft)	①	34,900	34,900	34,900	40,300	34,900	35,500
COMBAT RANGE (n mi)	③	---	---	---	---	---	2161
COMBAT RADIUS (n mi)	③	887	---	1010	350	642	---
Average speed (kn)		1721	---	1721	1721	1185	550
Initial cruising altitude (ft)		59,000	---	59,000	73,500	72,000	37,100
Final cruising altitude (ft)		76,000	---	76,000	76,400	76,000	45,300
Total mission time (hr)		1.20	---	1.43	0.68	2.34	3.92
TOTAL MISSION TIME (hr)	③	---	3.2	---	---	---	---
Interception altitude (ft)		---	77,400	---	---	---	---
COMBAT WEIGHT (lb)		78,118	86,253	74,543	66,190	71,283	58,274
Combat altitude (ft)		79,400 ①	77,400 ①	72,300 ①	74,500 ①	73,100 ①	48,300 ②
Combat speed (kn)		1721	1721	1721	1721	1721	1435
Combat climb (fpm)		500	500	14,350	14,750	14,500	74,430
Combat ceiling (500 fpm) (ft)	①	79,400	77,400	80,250	82,350	81,650	84,400
Combat ceiling (1.2g) (ft)	①	76,350	73,900	77,900	79,350	77,900	81,650
Service ceiling (100 fpm) (ft)	①	80,100	77,500	80,400	82,500	81,200	84,600
Service ceiling (one engine out) (ft)	①	42,000	39,200	42,500	44,800	43,400	47,000
Max rate of climb at SL (fpm)	①	44,000	39,600	45,000	50,700	47,000	57,500
Time: 36,152 ft & 94M to 70,000 ft & 3.0M (min)	①	4.1	4.9	4.0	3.5	3.8	8.0
Max speed at optimum altitude (kn/ft)	①	1721/76,550	1721/73,900	1721/77,000	1721/78,350	1721/77,000	1721/81,650
Basic speed at 50,000 ft (kn)		1526	1526	1526	1526	1526	1526
LANDING WEIGHT (lb)		50,893	58,331	59,018	57,905	59,018	58,274
Ground roll at SL (ft)	⑦	2030	1940	1960	1930	1960	1940
Total from 50 ft (ft)	⑦	3350	3230	3260	3220	3260	3230
Touchdown speed (kn)		133	130	131	130	131	130
Stall speed (kn)		93	91	91	90	91	91
Wing loading (psf)		32.5	31.3	31.7	31.1	31.7	31.3

NOTES

① Maximum power
② Military power
③ Detailed descriptions of RADIUS and RANGE missions given on page 6.
④ Allows for weight reduction during ground operation and climb.
⑤ Allows 0.8 min for take-off and acceleration to best climb speed.
⑥ Allows 1.2 min for take-off and acceleration to best climb speed
⑦ With 32.5% military thrust reverser.

PERFORMANCE BASIS:
(a) Data source: Estimated
(b) Performance is based on powers shown on page 5.

F-108A   S E C R E T   12 JUN 59

APPENDIX V

USAF F-108A 'BLACK BOOK' MISSION FORMULAS 12 JUNE 1959

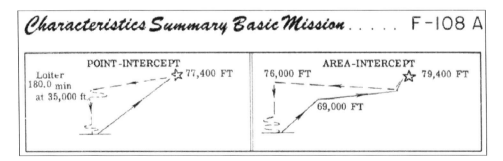

APPENDIX VI

CHARACTERISTIC SUMMARY BASIC MISSION F-108A
MOCK-UP PHASE 1959

Characteristics Summary Basic Mission F-108A

POINT-INTERCEPT	AREA-INTERCEPT
Loiter 180.0 min at 35,000 ft. ☆ 77,400 FT	76,000 FT ☆ 79,400 FT 69,000 FT

Note: The Appendix charts have been reproduced from the USAF 'Black Book' summary for the various North American NA-257 - F-108A iterations.

GLOSSARY

ADC	Air Defense Command
AIM	Airborne Interception Missile
ANG	Air National Guard
B	Bomber
BROFICON	Broadcast Fighter Control
C/D	Convergent/Divergent
DEW	Distant Early Warning
F	Fighter
FIS	Fighter Interception Squadron
fpm	feet per minute
ft	feet
Gal	Gallon
GAR	Guided Air Rocket
GE	General Electric
HF	High Frequency
lb.	Pound
ICBM	Inter-Continental Ballistic Missile
Knots	Nautical miles
Max	Maximum
Mil	Military
NA	North American
Nor	Normal
SAC	Strategic Air Command
SAGE	Semi-Automatic Ground Environment
TACAN	Tactical Air Navigation
USAF	United States Air Force
UHF	Ultra High Frequency
USN	United States Navy
XB	Experimental Bomber
XF	Experimental Fighter
YF	Development Fighter

BIBLIOGRAPHY

North American Report Nr. NA-58-84 "Performance Substantiation for the F-108A Primary Air Vehicle Weapon System 202A Contract AF33 (600)35603", dated 7 March 1958; Revised 15 December 1958

North American Report Nr. NA-59-506 "Performance Substantiation for the F-108A Primary Air Vehicle Weapon System 202A Contract AF33 (600)35605", dated 15 March 1959

USAF Black Book Characteristic documents for the North American NA-257 (F-108A) dated 2 May 1958, 1 October 1958, 15 December 1958 and 12 June 1959

In addition many other documents ranging from single page to several tens of pages were consulted from a number of sources including the USAF, NASA and its forebear NACA and North American and its successors.

ABOUT THE AUTHOR

Hugh, a historian and author, has published in excess of thirty books; non-fiction and fiction, writing under his own name as well as utilizing two different pseudonyms. He has also written for several international magazines, whilst his work has been used as reference for many other projects ranging from the aviation industry, international news corporations, film media to encyclopedias and the computer gaming industry. He currently resides in his native Scotland.

Other titles by the Author include

Boeing X-36 - Tailless Agility Flight Research Aircraft
X-32 - The Boeing Joint Strike Fighter
X-35 - Progenitor to the F-35 Lightning II
X-45 - Uninhabited Combat Air Vehicle
XF-92 - Convair's Arrow
Hurricane IIB Combat Log -151 Wing RAF North Russia 1941
RAF Meteor Jet Fighters in World War II, An Operational Log
Typhoon IA/B Combat Log - Operation Jubilee - August 1942
Defiant MK.I Combat Log - Fighter Command - May-September 1940
Tomahawk I/II Combat Log - European Theatre - 1941-42
Eurofighter Typhoon - Storm over Europe
Tornado F.2/F.3 Air Defence Variant
F-84 Thunderjet - Republic Thunder
USAF Jet Powered Fighters - XP-59-XF-85
British Battlecruisers of World War 1 - Operational Log, July 1914-June 1915
The Battle Cruiser Fleet at Jutland
Light Battlecruisers and the 2nd Battle of Heligoland Bight
Saab Gripen - The Nordic Myth
American Teens
Dassault Rafale – The Gallic Squall
Boeing F/A-18E/F Super Hornet

29887949R00030

Made in the USA
San Bernardino, CA
31 January 2016